MW01488891

BITCOIN

FOR BEGINNERS

The complete guide in
Blockchain bitcoin and the basic
Introduction Step-by-step to
earn money

2 book of 6

BY Luk Brandon Smith and
Mary Clark

Introduction:

Bitcoin is a sort of digital cash that is independent of customary banking and came into a spread in 2009. According to a bit of the top online sellers, Bitcoin is considered the most famous progressed cash that relies upon PC associations to handle complex mathematical issues. The Bitcoin trading scale doesn't depend upon the public bank and there is no single position that controls the load of Cryptocurrency. In any case, the Bitcoin cost depends upon the level of sureness its customers have, as the huger associations recognize Bitcoin as a procedure for installment, the more compelling Bitcoin will transform into.

The Bitcoin market is worldwide and the inhabitants of China and Japan have been particularly powerful in their purchase close by other Asian countries. Regardless, actually, in Bitcoin news, the Chinese government has endeavored to smother its development around there. That action drove the value of Bitcoin down for a short period yet it in a little while overwhelmed back and is as of now close to its past regard.

Bitcoin mining implies the cycle by which new Bitcoin is made. With customary cash, the public authority picks when and where to print and circle it. With Bitcoin, "backhoes" utilize remarkable programming to handle complex mathematical issues and are given a particular number of Bitcoin subsequently.

The most un-requesting way is apparently to get it through a high-level asset exchange like the as of late referred to Coinbase. Opening a record with them is easy and once you interface your record with them you can buy and sell Bitcoin with no issue. This is likely moreover the best spot to buy Bitcoins. One ought to comprehend what a Bitcoin wallet is and how to utilize it. It is exactly what might measure up to monetary equilibrium. It licenses you to get Bitcoins, store them and send them to others.

What it does is store a grouping of Bitcoin insurance keys. Commonly, it is mixed with a mysterious word or regardless safeguarded from unapproved access. There are a couple of sorts of current wallets to investigate. A web wallet licenses you to send, get and store Bitcoin anyway your web program. Another sort is a work territory wallet and here the wallet writing computer programs is taken care of clearly on your PC. There are furthermore flexible wallets that are planned for use by a PDA.

Chapter: 1

There's virtual money, and afterward, there's Bitcoin. The super quirky Bitcoin is a numerically determined money that vows to change how people use money. Bitcoins are not genuine coins-they're strings of code bolted with military-grade encryption-and people who use them to purchase and sell labor and products are hard to follow.

There's something to be said about utilizing the money that isn't managed by the public authority or banks, doesn't accompany the typical exchange expenses, and is difficult to fake. Bitcoin likewise vows to be catastrophe verification, since you can't annihilate numbers similarly that you can obliterate gold saves or paper money.

Bitcoin is digital money made in 2009 by a designer covering up under the nom de plume Satoshi Nakamoto (apparently a Japanese person who has ideal order of American English). Bitcoin is decentralized, which means it isn't constrained by a focal power like a monetary foundation, nation, government, or person. It is shared and open-source, circulated across the web from one PC to another, without the need for brokers.

Contrasted with U.S. dollars, Bitcoin is untraceable, making it alluring to libertarians scared of government intruding and inhabitants of the hidden world. You can utilize it to pay for buys online and off, from illicit medications on the Silk Road to genuine eatery suppers.

How Bitcoin becomes very significant is that there is a limited quantity in presence. There will just at any point be a limit of 21 million Bitcoins and not at all like ordinary fiat monetary standards you can't simply print a greater amount of them at whatever point you feel like. This is because Bitcoin runs on a proof of work convention: to make it, you have to mine it utilizing PC handling ability to address complex calculations on the Bitcoin blockchain.

Whenever this is accomplished, you are remunerated with Bitcoin as an installment for the "work" you have done. Lamentably, the prize you get for mining has diminished pretty much consistently since Bitcoin's commencement, which implies that for a great many people the solitary suitable approach to get Bitcoin is getting it on a trade. At the current worth levels is that a danger worth taking?

Bitcoins enjoy a few huge benefits:

1: The receipt and installment measure is impartial, straightforward, and unsurprising.

2: Processing doesn't cost any expenses or truth be told, little charges.

3: You can send and get boundless measures of money immediately whenever to and from anyplace on the planet.

4: Bitcoin exchanges are irreversible, which shields dealers from the fake chargebacks that are progressively regular with Mastercards.

5: Payments are made without personal data being traded, which gives solid security against fraud.

Nonetheless, utilizing bitcoins has a few disservices:

1: Their worth is unpredictable because the quantity of bitcoins available for use is tiny so moderately little exchanges can influence their cost essentially.

2: They are not yet acknowledged generally and accordingly can't be utilized all over the place.

You can get Bitcoins from companions, online giveaways, or by getting them with genuine money from Bitcoin trades.

Utilizing genuine money to purchase Bitcoins invalidates the general purpose of namelessness, in any case, since you may have to add your ledger to an outsider site. You can likewise purchase Bitcoins by the use of any cell phone OR money store foundations.

New Bitcoins are made by "mining." Mining is done consequently by PCs or workers it's not certifiable mining where you need to burrow underground to uncover wares, yet the idea is comparable. You should apply energy to uncover gold. You should also invest asset and time to record and check Bitcoin exchanges.

Perhaps the coolest thing about Bitcoin is that it gets its worth not from certifiable things, but rather from codes. Bitcoins are pulled out of the ether by machines (and people who run them) in return for taking care of complex numerical issues identified with the current number of Bitcoins. These massive and expensive supercomputers accompany amazing encryption capacities.

In an average exchange, purchaser A structure area X pays dealer B some Bitcoins online. Diggers then the competition to confirm and scramble the exchange, logging Bitcoin codes in a focal worker. Whoever settles the riddle initially gets the Bitcoins. Around 25 new Bitcoins are made for each 10-minute square, however, that number can increment or abatement relying upon how long the organization runs.

Bitcoin's Work as an Unidentified Payment Processor

You can complete 3 things with bitcoins, you can make a buy, send money namelessly to somebody or use it as a venture. By using bitcoins rather than money, you are making that buy namelessly. The same thing goes for sending money, in light of the way that you don't need to present a heap of installment with the goal for you to build up a bitcoin secretly, basically you can send money to another person namelessly.

Instructions to Setup an Account

You can gain a bitcoin wallet from a bitcoin dealer like Coinbase. At the point when you open up a wallet through a confirmed representative, you are given a bitcoin address which is a progression of numbers and letters.

How Does Bitcoin Work as an Investment?

The cost of a bitcoin changes now and then. Just to place things in context, back at the start of 2013, the normal cost of a bitcoin was roughly $400 per bitcoin. This implied that if you had 2 bitcoins worth $800 at the start of 2013 and you put away it as a venture before the finish of 2013 those two bitcoins will value $2000 plus rather than $800. Numerous people store bitcoins because of their way that the worth vacillates.

How Do You Send Bitcoin?

With the goal for you to pay for labor and products or to send bitcoins to a person, 3 things are required. Your private key, bitcoin address, & the person's bitcoin address. Starting there, through your bitcoin wallet, you will put 3 snippets of data, which are: info, equilibrium, and yield. Information alludes to your location, balance alludes to the measure of bitcoins you will send, and yield is the beneficiary's location.

Bitcoin Anonymity

While doing a bitcoin exchange, there's no compelling reason to give the genuine name of the person. Every single one of the bitcoin exchanges is recorded is the thing that is known as a public log. This log contains just wallet IDs and not people's names. so essentially every exchange is private. People can purchase and sell things without being followed.

Storing and Saving Bitcoins

These bitcoins are put away in what is called digital wallets. These wallets exist in the cloud or people's PCs. A wallet is a comparable thing to a virtual ledger. These wallets help all people to get or send bitcoins, pay or simply save the bitcoins. Gone against financial balances, these bitcoin wallets are never safeguarded by the FDIC.

Bitcoin Advancement

Bitcoin set up a different method of development. The bitcoin software is open-source. Anybody can survey it. These days' actuality is that bitcoin is changing the world's funds like how the web significantly altered distributing. The idea is splendid. Novel thoughts show up when everybody approaches the bitcoin worldwide. Exchange expenses decrease is a reality of bitcoin. Tolerating bitcoins cost anything, likewise, they're not difficult to arrange. Chargebacks don't exist. The bitcoin local area will produce extra organizations, however.

Bitcoin Casino and Poker Sites

The betting business has taken up bitcoin as an installment strategy. It is because of the namelessness of bitcoin. Both bitcoin club and bitcoin poker locales are springing up and offering their players to set aside installments, play with bitcoin at the tables and pull out straightforwardly to their bitcoin wallet. It means there are no opportunities or duties for government control. Similar to a standard Nevada gambling club where do you don't have to enroll anyplace and every one of your exchanges is mysterious.

5 Merits of Bitcoins That You Didn't Know

As a new and developing virtual money, Bitcoin enjoys certain unmistakable upper hands over the regular government-level monetary standards. By using Bitcoin, you can have the following advantages:

1: Flexible Online Payments

Bitcoin is an online installment framework and like some other such framework, the clients of Bitcoin have the advantage of paying for their coins from any side of the world that has a web association. This implies that you could be lying on your bed and buying coins as opposed to taking the torment of making a trip to a particular bank or store to complete your work. In addition, an online installment through Bitcoin doesn't expect you to fill in insights regarding your data. Consequently, Bitcoin preparing Bitcoin exchanges is much less complex than those brought out through U.S. Financial balances and Mastercards.

2: No Taxation

At the point when you make buys using dollars, euros, or some other government level money, you need to pay an expansion amount of money to the public authority as an expense. All things have their own assessment rate. Nonetheless, when you're making a buy through Bitcoin, deals charges are not added to your buy. This is considered an authoritative document of tax avoidance and is one of the significant benefits of being a Bitcoin client. Even with zero expense rates, it can be very useful mainly when buying extravagance things that are discerning to an unknown land. Such things, usually, are vigorously burdened by the public authority.

3: Minimal Transaction Fees

Expenses and trade costs are a vital part of standard wire moves and worldwide buys. Bitcoin isn't checked or directed by any mediator organization or government office. Accordingly, the expenses of executing are kept extremely low dissimilar to global exchanges made using customary monetary standards. Moreover, exchanges in Bitcoin are not known to be tedious since it doesn't include the inconveniences of commonplace approval necessities and holding up periods.

4: No External Intercessions

Perhaps the best benefit of Bitcoin is that it disposes of outsider interferences. This implies that administrations, banks, and other monetary middle people have no authority at all to upset client exchanges or freeze a Bitcoin account. As referenced previously, Bitcoin depends rigorously on a shared situation. Henceforth, the clients of Bitcoin appreciate more noteworthy freedom when causing buys with Bitcoins than they do when utilizing traditional public monetary standards.

5: Concealed User Identity

All Bitcoin exchanges are distinct. Bitcoin gives you the alternative of user mystery. Bitcoins are like money just buys as in your exchanges can never be followed back to you and these buys are never associated with your personality. In actuality, the Bitcoin address that is made for client buys is never something very similar for two unique exchanges. If you need to, you do have the choice of deliberately uncovering and distributing your Bitcoin exchanges however by and large clients stay discreet.

How to Use Bitcoins?

You should store Bitcoin in an online wallet when you get your hands on some of them. You can do it through a PC program or an outcast site. You will become a part of the Bitcoin network. It will be when you will make your virtual wallet. To send Bitcoins to another client or pay for online buys, get that person/merchant's ID number and move Bitcoins online. Handling requires around a couple of moments to 60 minutes, as Bitcoin diggers across the globe check the exchange.

In case you're as yet wary, one Bitcoin is presently worth about $90 (starting at 18 April 2013), with hourly variances that can make an informal investor bleary-eyed. Unpredictable, however, an ever-increasing number of people are beginning to drain the marvel for all it is worthwhile it keeps going. How to get your cut of the virtual dash for unheard of wealth? A few different ways: Sell Bitcoin mining PCs, sell your Bitcoins at insane costs on eBay and theorize on Bitcoin markets.

You can likewise begin mining. Any person can mine Bitcoins, yet except if you can manage the cost of a proficient arrangement, it will take a normal PC a year or more to tackle calculations.

Bitcoins are exchanged secretly absurdly, with no interest concerning set up monetary establishments. Starting in 2012, deals of medications and other underground market merchandise represented an expected 20 percent of trades from bitcoins to U.S. dollars. The Drug Enforcement Agency as of late directed its first-since forever Bitcoin seizure, after purportedly tying an exchange on the unknown Bitcoin-just commercial center Silk Road to the offer of solution and unlawful medications.

Some Bitcoin clients have likewise proposed that the money can fill in as a way to keep away from charges. That might be valid, yet just as bitcoins help unlawful tax avoidance, not as in they serve any part in real expense arranging. Under government charge law, no money needs to change submits a request for an available exchange to happen. Deal and other non-money trades are still completely available. There is no explanation that exchanges including bitcoins would be dealt with unexpectedly.

Outside of the criminal component, Bitcoin's primary enthusiasts are theorists, who do not expect utilizing bitcoins to purchase anything. These financial backers are persuaded that the restricted inventory of bitcoins will compel their worth to follow a consistent vertical direction.

So, if Bitcoin is quite pointless as real money, what are its applications? Many trust Bitcoin has proceeded onward from being a practical type of installment to turning into a store of significant worth. Bitcoin resembles "digital gold" and will be utilized as a benchmark for other digital currencies and blockchain ventures to be estimated against and exchanged for. As of late, there have been accounts of people in high expansion nations, for example, Zimbabwe purchasing Bitcoin to clutch what abundance they have as opposed to seeing its worth decrease under the wildness of its focal financial framework.

Do you want to learn where is it possible to engage in Bitcoin? If you trust in how these digital forms of money will help the world, it is never past the point where it is possible to get included, yet with the expense of Bitcoin being so high is it a boat for some which have effectively cruised. You may be in an ideal situation viewing Lite coin, up 6908% for the year, or Ethereum which is up an amazing 7521% for the year. These more current, quicker monetary standards desire to accomplish what Bitcoin first set off to do move in quite a while beginning in 2009 and supplant government-run fiat monetary standards.

Online Bitcoin Trading

Understanding Bitcoin and The Block-Chain

Bitcoin is a distributed installment framework, also called electronic money or virtual money. It offers 21st century option as compared to physical banking. Trades are made using "e-wallet programming". Bitcoin has undermined the conventional financial framework while working outside of unofficial laws.

Bitcoin utilizes modern cryptography, can be given in any partial category, and has a decentralized dispersion framework, is popular worldwide, and offers a few unmistakable benefits over different monetary forms like the US dollar.

For one, it can never be embellished or frozen by the bank(s) or an administration office. Back in 2009, when the bitcoin was worth only ten pennies for each coin, you would have transformed 1,000 dollars into millions, if you stood by only eight years.

By removing the banks from the condition, you are likewise killing a lot of every exchange charge. Moreover, the measure of time needed to move money from direct A toward point B is decreased considerably.

The biggest exchange at any point that occurs utilizing bitcoin is one hundred and fifty million dollars. This exchange occurred in seconds with negligible fees. To move enormous amounts of money utilizing a "confided-in outsider", would require days and cost hundreds if not a great many dollars. This clarifies why the banks are fiercely against people purchasing, selling, exchanging, moving, and spending bitcoins. Only.003% of the universe's (250,000) populace is assessed to hold in any event one bitcoin. Also, just 24% of the populace understand what it is. Bitcoin exchanges are entered sequentially in a 'blockchain' simply the way bank exchanges are. Squares, in the interim, resemble singular bank explanations.

Setting up Your E Wallet Software Account

When you make your one-of-a-kind e-wallet programming account, you will move assets from your e-wallet to a beneficiaries' e-wallet, like bitcoin. If you might want to utilize a bitcoin ATM to pull out assets from your record you will interface your e-wallet 'address to the picked ATM's e-wallet 'address'.

To work with the exchange of your assets in bitcoin to and from an exchanging stage, you will just connect your e-wallet 'address to the e-wallet 'address' of your picked exchanging stage. It is a lot simpler than it sounds. The expectation to absorb information comparable to utilizing your e-wallet is exceptionally short. To set up an e-wallet, there are a bunch of organizations online that offer protected, secure, free, and turn-key e-wallet arrangements.

A straightforward Google search will help you track down the correct e-wallet programming for you, contingent on what your requirements are actually. Numerous people begin utilizing a "blockchain" account. This is extremely secure. You have the alternative of setting up a two-level login convention, to additional improve the wellbeing and security, according to your e-wallet account, basically shielding your record from being hacked into.

It is a protected spot for your bitcoin and other digital monetary forms. To pull out money in your nearby money, from your e-wallet, you are needed to find a bitcoin ATM, which can frequently be found in neighborhood organizations inside the most significant urban communities.

Buy Any Fractional Denomination of Bitcoin

To purchase any measure of bitcoin, you are needed to manage a digital money merchant. Likewise, with any money merchant, you should pay the intermediary a charge, when you buy your bitcoin. It is feasible to buy.1 of bitcoin or less if that is all that you might want to buy. The expense is founded on the current market worth of a full bitcoin at some random time.

There is a bunch of bitcoin dealers online. A straightforward Google search will permit you to handily source out the best one for you. It is a good idea to contrast their rates before with ongoing with a buy. You ought to likewise affirm the pace of a bitcoin online, preceding making a buy through a representative, as the rate will in general vary much of the time.

Avoid Any Trading Platform Promising Unrealistic Returns to Unsuspecting Investors

Tracking down a legitimate bitcoin exchanging organization that offers an exceptional yield is vital to your online achievement. Procuring 1% each day is viewed as an exceptional yield in this industry. Procuring 10% each day is unthinkable. With online bitcoin exchanging, it is plausible to twofold your advanced money inside ninety days. You should try not to be attracted by any organization that is offering returns, for example, 10% each day. This kind of return isn't practical with digital money exchanging. There is an organization considered Coinexpro that was offering 10% each day to bitcoin dealers.

Furthermore, it wound up being a Ponzi conspire. If it's 10% each day, leave. The previously mentioned exchanging stage had all the earmarks of being extremely complex and seemed to be being authentic. My recommendation is to zero in on exchanging your bitcoin with an organization that offers sensible returns, for example, 1% each day. There will be different organizations that will endeavor to isolate you from your bitcoin utilizing deceitful techniques. Be extremely careful with regards to any organization that is offering ridiculous returns.

When you move your bitcoin to a recipient, there is no way to get it back. You should guarantee that your picked exchanging organization is completely digital and coordinated with blockchain, from receipt to installment. All the more critically, it is significant that you figure out how to separate genuine exchanging openings from deceitful "company's" that are specialists with regards to isolating its customers from their money. The bitcoin and other advanced monetary forms are not the issues. It is the exchanging stages that you should practice alert with, preceding giving over your well-deserved money.

However, Your ROI should likewise be naturally moved into your "e-wallet" at customary stretches, all through your agreement term. There is 1 stage that is great to use. It pays each bitcoin financial backer/broker 1.1% each day in revenue just as 1.1% each day in the capital. This kind of return is faltering contrasted with what you would acquire with conventional monetary business sectors, notwithstanding, with digital currency, it is normal. Most banks will payout 2% each year.

If you are needed to direct monotonous exercises like signing into your record, sending messages, tapping on joins, and so on, you unquestionably need to continue looking for a reasonable exchanging organization that offers a set-it-and-forget-it sort of stage, as they exist.

How to Use a Bitcoin Generator?

First of all, you should open the bitcoin software on your PC screen. Presently interface it to your web worker, as it is gotten and mysterious you can undoubtedly create or twofold your concern with no difficulty. So the primary advance in multiplying your bitcoin is to initially store the entirety. For storing the money, you need to enter your bitcoin wallet address in the store bar. Presently your wallet window is opened, from that point move your aggregate to the store bar.

For this reason, click on the send catch and glue your bitcoin store address to send the money to the bitcoin programming for multiplying your sum. You will see a warning of a fruitful installment move in your bitcoin programming window. Presently, this bitcoin money will get changed over into the product money, following a couple of moments the sum will be multiplied consequently. Presently click the catch store, to see the sum saved and the money multiplied. A while later snap on the catch invigorate, to get the full rundown of your exchange, for instance, if you saved 0.10 bitcoins the sum multiplied will be 0.20 bitcoins in your wallet.

Presently to pull out your bitcoin money, you need to go to your bitcoin wallet, from that point click on get catch and duplicate the location flying on your window. The subsequent stage is to glue the location on the pull-out bitcoin bar and snap the pull-out button. The entire interaction will take some time, however, after the fulfillment, you will see a notice flying on your screen expressing "Bitcoin got" and bitcoins will show up on your wallet.

A bitcoin generator is a basic method of bringing in simple money. Bitcoin capacities are based on the cryptographic convention. Bitcoins are the image of money through which the client makes the exchange of getting and sending the money in bitcoins rather than genuine money. Bitcoin generators are programming that duplicates or triples your bitcoins in 5 to 10 minutes with insignificant equilibrium in your bitcoin wallet. Numerous organizations are offering a free bitcoin generator, however, before contributing do the exhaustive exploration as large numbers of them are fakes. Bitcoin is the new money for the new age and has a wide degree in the coming future.

Things You Can Do with Bitcoin

You will want to exchange, execute, acknowledge and store bitcoin. You can send it to your companions, demand it from a companion, and store it in your digital wallet. Exchange cost is low as compared to Credit cards, PayPal, and some other online mediators. Moreover, it additionally secures your protection that may get spilled online while utilizing Visas. It is very secure. No one can take or seize coins.

Because of its straightforwardness in the framework, it is additionally unrealistic to control as a result of the common public record. You can confirm exchange from any place and whenever. The request is probably going to ascend as the all-out creation of bitcoins is to be restricted to 21 million in particular. Japan has effectively authorized it and different nations may follow it soon and the cost may climb further.

I will cover more on Bitcoins in detail in the forthcoming days where you will learn incredible stuff about bitcoin exchanging. You can remark your perspectives and ask anything applicable to bitcoins. If you discovered this current fledgling manual for Bitcoin Cryptocurrency valuable, do share and like it on informal communities.

Is Bitcoin a Good Investment?

There are a few significant contrasts between Bitcoin and customary monetary standards (for example U.S. dollar):

Bitcoin is made through a cycle called "Bitcoin mining". Excavators throughout the planet use mining programming and PCs to tackle complex bitcoin calculations and to favor Bitcoin exchanges. They are granted with exchange charges and new Bitcoins produced from addressing Bitcoin calculations.

A public record called 'Blockchain' records all Bitcoin exchanges and shows each Bitcoin proprietor's particular property. Anybody can get to the public record to check exchanges. This makes digital money more straightforward and unsurprising. All the more critically, the simply prevent extortion and twofold expenditure of similar Bitcoins.

There are limited Bitcoins available for use. As per Blockchain, there were about 12.1 million available for use as of Dec. 20, 2013. The trouble to mine Bitcoins (tackle calculations) gets more enthusiastically as more Bitcoins are created, and the greatest sum available for use is covered at 21 million. This makes Bitcoins more important as more people use them.

Bitcoin doesn't have an incorporated power or clearing house (for example government, a national bank, MasterCard, or Visa organization). The distributed installment network is overseen by clients and excavators throughout the planet. The money is namelessly moved straightforwardly between clients through the web without going through a clearinghouse. This implies that exchange expenses are a lot lower.

The digital money can be obtained through Bitcoin mining or Bitcoin trades.

Bitcoin wallets are used for Bitcoins, private keys, and public locations just as for secretly moving Bitcoins between clients. Digital money is acknowledged by a predetermined number of traders online and in some physical retailers.

Bitcoins are not insured by government offices. They are not secured. Subsequently, they can't be recuperated if the mysterious keys are taken by a programmer or lost to a bombed hard drive, or because of the conclusion of a Bitcoin trade. If the mysterious keys are lost, the related Bitcoins can't be recuperated and would be unavailable for general use. Visit this connection for a FAQ on Bitcoins.

How One Can Stay in The World of Bitcoins?

As bitcoins began to appear to an ever-increasing extent, people began to acknowledge them in return for true merchandise. When others saw that this was going on, they become roused to accomplish seriously mining. To tackle the numerical question speedier, greater, quicker PCs were required. Interests in server farm assets were made and what had been something that people were doing at home on spare PCs immediately become a mechanical activity practically overnight.

As product directors, if we need to have something to put on our product chief resume then, we must ensure that the organization is a triumph regardless of what product or administration we are selling. On account of a bitcoin digger, we're selling a mining administration that makes esteem basically by making more bitcoins. Something that we need to stay mindful of is the worth of bitcoins because as the worth goes down, the assets that we need to work with will be restricted.

The way that bitcoins are made is by having PCs take care of a numerical question. At the point when the numerical statement is settled, the organization will have gotten more bitcoins for our work. The test is that PCs are turning out to be quicker and quicker and that is permitting more contenders to go into this market.

As product administrators, we need to find ways to ensure that the organization can help our ability and increase the processing assets. At this moment the universe of bitcoins is similar to a disrupted outskirt. The principles have not yet been composed; however, there is a lot of money to be acquired. Product chiefs have a significant task to carry out in staying with them that they work for above water by watching what's new with bitcoin trade rates and ensuring that the bitcoin mining limit is being expanded.

Chapter: 2

Have you found out about bitcoins? It's the craziest thing - people are in the process of composing their item improvement definition and concocting pristine money. This cash has no connections to any government or country. The entire thing "lives" in the personalities of the Computer who together make up the Internet. The math behind it is a touch complex, yet it is by all accounts filling in prevalence and, all the more critically, you can purchase things utilizing bitcoins.

So what's everything about?

Bitcoin is a type of money equivalent to some other, anyway, it isn't heavily influenced by any government or financial establishment. The reason is for it to be claimed and overseen by its local area. Bitcoin is de-incorporated and overseen by distributed people who all participate in new exchange movements and store past action in what is known as 'block chains'.

This implies that a full 'duplicate' of all exchanges are put away locally and used to check, between members, new movement, accordingly keeping any one person from deforming, adding, or making counterfeit exchanges inside the square chain. Bitcoin works in not a disparate manner to PayPal in that you have a computerized wallet with a unique location where people can send you Bitcoins. You can essentially introduce a wallet on your gadget, or you can download the full Bitcoin wallet and partake in the organization as a hub.

Maybe then being controlled by a solitary body, bitcoin is a decentralized distributed cash, implying that it lives on the PC of everybody that works with it. (Equivalent to the actual web.) Given that it's decentralized, nobody can ruin the commercial center by delivering more bitcoins into dissemination and no divider road financier is filling one's pockets by lasting in the center of each request.

The advantages of bitcoin are that exchanges happen in a split second and don't need an exchange expense - except if the person beginning the exchange chooses to pay one. Since no one controls the bitcoin network, there are Computers throughout the world who help affirm every exchange that occurs - this interaction is classified as "mining.".

To boost these "diggers" to help validate every one of the exchanges, the bitcoin network awards bitcoins to excavators sporadically. Eventually, 25 bitcoins are compensated in a type of lottery system like clockwork. The program behind bitcoin manages this lottery and it's open-source so everybody can see it.

The rate that bitcoins are granted will divide to 12.5 in 2017 and afterward cut down the middle again at regular intervals until the last bitcoins are remunerated in 2140. Then, there will be an aggregate of 21 million bitcoins around and that is it- - no more will at any point be made. In light of the current conversion standard, there are more than $1.4 billion bitcoins on the lookout.

The way bitcoin bargains work is extremely essential, everybody has a bitcoin wallet that they use to send and acquire reserves. This wallet is a basic series of letters and numbers, helping make that wallet completely private except if the person decides to interface themselves with it. The private substance of bitcoin bargains has caused it to be utilized for an assortment of illegal exercises. While denied buys may occur, there are a large number of foundations, projects, and economies everywhere in the world that perceive bitcoin.

A portion of Bitcoin's advantages may have problematic worth. The publicized advantages incorporate having the option to email your friend's cash, it is identified with gold, it offers security and soundness, and so forth. I tried two diverse Bitcoin wallet projects, and it appeared as though they would have required days to complete the process of planning things with Bitcoin's far-off worker organization.

Purchasing Bitcoins isn't modest. What's more, except eBay, purchasing Bitcoins isn't straightforward or simple; and aside from (presumably) EBay, a portion of the Bitcoin merchants appear to be somewhat flaky. For a test, I messaged four Bitcoin trade merchants, including two fairly near me, and none of them reacted. There are no discounts at the time of purchasing Bitcoins.

With Bitcoin, the odds of getting ripped off for buys unfathomably increments, because practically no dealer data is imparted to the purchaser, like their name and address.

I would figure that because Bitcoins are thoroughly secure and private, and because they can be utilized to purchase anything anyplace, utilizing them may help get you on the public authority's radar. Who knows, perhaps that person selling unobtainium that you can just purchase with Bitcoins, is really with some police division, hoping to bust you.

Bitcoin Wallets
What is a bitcoin wallet?

A Bitcoin wallet is a product program where you can store bitcoins securely. A wallet is like a virtual ledger and permits the person to send or get bitcoins and save the bitcoins. Those people who use bitcoin and have a balance, get a private key or mystery number for each bitcoin address which is saved in the bitcoin wallet. Bitcoin exchange is unimaginable without the private key. You can utilize your Bitcoin wallet from any place on the planet.

The principle explanation for getting a bitcoin stockpiling wallet is to utilize bitcoin effectively and securely. It is an advanced wallet that can run effectively on your PC & PDA gadgets. Assuming you are worried about hacking, it is the most ideal alternative since it gives full security and wellbeing of your bitcoin.

Various Types of a Bitcoin Wallet

Here are the types of a bitcoin wallet. Every one of them can be used according to their prerequisites.

The four primary kinds of a bitcoin wallet are as referenced as underneath:

• **Web**

Web wallets permit you to utilize bitcoins from any place effectively and on any portable or internet browser. Keep in mind, you should pick your web wallet cautiously because it stores your private key online and it tends to be unsafe now and then.

• **Mobile**

The people who are utilizing bitcoins consistently, for example, routinely exchanging, purchasing merchandise, and all the more day by day exercises, the Mobile BTC wallet is an extraordinary alternative. It is an application that runs on your PDA.

• **Hardware**

Equipment wallets store your private keys disconnected so they can't be hacked. This implies you can utilize it at whatever point you need on your PC.

• **Desktop**

Work area wallets are downloaded and introduced on your PC or work area and offer you unlimited authority over the wallet.

Bitcoins are sovereign with their unmistakable standards and aren't imprinted covertly by any bank however mined, they're created carefully by a decent number of people engaged with a giant organization or local area.

Diggers for the most part utilize colossal processing power, and a lot of rivalries are engaged with Bitcoin mining. Computer work to take care of complex numerical issues. The contending diggers additionally can procure Bitcoins simultaneously, simply by taking care of the issue. Although trouble levels of these issues are getting serious step by step.

Exchanges at the Bitcoin network are constant and unremitting, and monitoring those exchanges is genuinely precise. Bitcoin network keeps it systematic, as, during a given period, all exchanges are gathered in a square. The diggers should approve exchanges, and everything is recorded in an overall record, which is an assortment of squares, named blockchain. Blockchain holds the way into the subtleties of any exchange made across different Bitcoin addresses.

Bitcoin joining into people's lives is the most desired thing at present. Bitcoin devotees can have a lot of decisions when they are hoping to obtain this advanced money. A Bitcoin trade empowers buyers to purchase or sell Bitcoins by utilizing fiat financial forms.

Trades are of great value. With trades, customers can buy or sell Bitcoins with wired exchanges, money, or credit/check card installment. Excitement and a tireless furor consistently go with Bitcoins. With various fans who are quick to exchange Bitcoins, the youthful money and all the fever encompassing it appears to grow somewhat consistently. All the information related to it is by all accounts as significant as the actual cash. The meaning of a "Bitcoin wiki", a self-sufficient task, can't be denied by any stretch of the imagination. It will go about as a storage facility of information for Bitcoin devotees from one side of the planet to the other.

What About Having a Bitcoin Wallet On PC?

You will see a field where you can reorder a number like this from a person you need to send cash to and off it will go straightforwardly into that person's wallet. You can even make a QR code that will allow somebody to snap a photo with an application on their telephone and send you some bitcoin. It is protected to give these out - the location and QR code are both for my gifts page. Go ahead and give.

This sort of wallet acts both as a wallet for you and as a feature of the bitcoin system. Bitcoin works explain that each exchange is communicated and recorded as a number across the whole system (implying that each exchange is affirmed and made irreversible by the actual organization). Any PC with the correct programming can be essential for that system, checking and supporting the organization. This wallet fills in as your wallet and as a help for that system. Also, know that it will take up 8-9 gigabytes of your PC's memory.

What Makes Bitcoin So Volatile?

Merchants are constantly worried about 'Bitcoin's unpredictability. It is critical to understand what makes the worth of this specific computerized cash profoundly precarious. Actually like numerous different things, the worth of 'Bitcoin' likewise relies on the principles of interest and supply. If the interest for 'Bitcoin' expands, the cost will likewise increment.

Unexpectedly side, the abatement popular for the 'Bitcoin' will prompt diminished interest. Assuming countless people wish to buy 'Bitcoin's, the cost will rise. If more people need to sell 'Bitcoin's, the cost will descend.

It merits realizing that the worth of 'Bitcoin' can be unstable whenever contrasted with more settled wares and financial forms. After being prodded in late 2016, 'Bitcoin' contacted another record undeniable level in the principal seven-day stretch of the current year. There could be a few components causing 'Bitcoin' to be unpredictable. A portion of these is talked about here.

For What Reason Do I Require Bitcoin News?

The cost has generally been unstable, with huge pinnacles and droops at stretches. As of late, the cost of a Bitcoin jumped up more than 10-crease in only two months. In 2013 a few Bitcoin Millionaires were made for the time being the point at which the worth of their Bitcoin wallets expanded significantly.

If you as of now hold some bitcoins in your computerized wallet or are considering trying things out, then you truly should keep up to speed with the Bitcoin News. Exchanging Bitcoin is an inexorably famous other option or extra to regular unfamiliar trade exchanging, and is filling in help as more representatives dive in.

Notwithstanding the progressively falling pace of Bitcoin revelation, the interest in Bitcoin news proceeds.

Bitcoin got solid support from PayPal as of late which will surely reinforce trust in its believability as a dependable option in contrast to a regular bank card or money exchanges online and the high road. This may go some approach to mollify the pundits of Bitcoin, who guarantee that the system used to favor or approve exchanges, called Blockchain, and is unstable and powerless against assault by programmers.

Variances of the Perceived Value

Another incredible justification for 'Bitcoin' worth becoming unstable is the variance of 'Bitcoin's apparent worth. This is managed by a plan chosen by the creators of the center innovation to confine its creation to a static sum, 21 million BTC. Because of this factor, financial backers may allot less or more resources into 'Bitcoin'.

The Bad Press Factor

'Bitcoin' users are for the most part frightened by various news occasions including the assertions by government authorities and international occasions that 'Bitcoin' can be directed. It implies the pace of 'Bitcoin' selection is grieved by negative or awful press reports. Diverse awful reports made dread in financial backers and precluded them from putting resources into this advanced money. An illustration of terrible feature news is the famous usage of 'Bitcoin' in handling drug exchanges through Silk Road which concluded with the FBI stoppage of the market in October 2013.

Such accounts delivered alarm among people and caused the 'Bitcoin' worth to diminish extraordinarily. On the opposite side, veterans in the exchanging business considered such to be episodes as proof that the 'Bitcoin' industry is developing. So the 'Bitcoin' began to acquire its expanded worth not long after the impact of the awful press disappeared.

News about Security Breaches

Different news offices and advanced media assume a significant part in building a negative or positive public idea. If you see something being publicized Advantageously, you are probably going to go for that without giving a lot of consideration to the negative sides. There has been news about 'Bitcoin' security breaks and it truly made the financial backers reconsider before putting their well-deserved cash in 'Bitcoin' exchanging. They become too powerless about picking a particular 'Bitcoin' venture stage.

'Bitcoin' may become unstable when the 'Bitcoin' people group uncovers security susceptibilities with an end goal to make an incredible open-source reaction in the type of safety fixes. Thusly, it is prudent that 'Bitcoin' engineers should open security weaknesses to the overall population to make solid arrangements.

Everybody is interested in what bitcoin is and how one will acquire it and spend it. Bitcoin is the most celebrated and greatest advanced cash on the planet in regards to showcase capitalization and the portion of the overall industry where there are no delegates to deal with the exchanges. Microsoft Co-organizer, Bill Gates has a ton of confidence in Bitcoin to the purpose of saying, "Bitcoin is an innovative masterpiece."

As per Leon Low, a Nobel Peace Prize candidate, each educated person has to know at any rate about bitcoin since it can get one of the world's most critical turns of events. One can purchase bitcoins straightforwardly from other bitcoin users using commercial centers or through trades, and one pays for them through hard money, credit or check cards, electronic wire moves, other digital currencies, PayPal, et al.

Get a Bitcoin Wallet

This is the first step when purchasing bitcoins. Diverse bitcoin wallets give changing degrees of safety, and you can pick the security level that turns out best for your exchanges. The most mainstream wallet choices are

• A multi-sig wallet

• An electronic help

• A wallet software

The subsequent stage is to subsidize your Bitcoin wallet and begin setting orders.

Where to Buy Bitcoins

Coinbase: - This is one more of the famous bitcoin wallets with perhaps the least difficult methods of purchasing bitcoin. Upon joining, one gets a $5 reward. It has a trust score of A+.

Localbitcoins: - This is the essential site for orchestrating up close and personal exchanges and costs arranged. Its escrow government has made the site famous since it adds a layer of assurance for the purchaser and the dealer with a trust score of A.

Bitquick: - This site is additionally fledgling agreeable permitting users to purchase and acknowledge installments

44

for bitcoins using hard cash just as the bank moves. It has a trust rating of B.

With bitcoins, you can secretly purchase stock; make less expensive worldwide installments since Bitcoins are not dependent upon guidelines from any country. The bitcoin market is exceptionally unstable and more people are getting them wanting to make a benefit when the cost goes up.

Albeit an online wallet is a helpful strategy for purchasing bitcoins there are a few different alternatives, for example, choosing a bitcoin dealer. It is likewise critical to pick the correct one as there are swindlers and one should be cautious about them. Though various setup trades offer the wallet governments to the users while searching for a bitcoin wallet system the person should choose the one that has a multi-signature office.

The users can likewise utilize the bitcoin trade search in the person's computer or cell phones and by putting some broad data, for example, composing one's nation name the person can find many trades in the world.

The users can likewise utilize the fluid cash they have since there are different choices accessible in the commercial center, for example, nearby bitcoin governments that assist the users to trade them with cash. Such regions permit the users to visit the closest bank office for keeping the money sum and get the bitcoins after at some point.

Numerous people accept that bitcoins address another time of advanced cash and frequently get mistaken for them.

However, since the bitcoin chain system is completely mechanized it is very basic and simple to purchase and utilize them particularly they are hellfire modest with regards to worldwide exchanges. Since trades request an assortment of installment cycles, for example, credit or charge cards, the buyers can likewise purchase online by opening a record based on the separate topographical area.

When the trades get the installments after confirmation they would save the bitcoins in the interest of the people and submit them in the particular wallets. For this, they charge a few expenses. The whole interaction may be tedious. Numerous people who are figuring out how to purchase bitcoins can likewise utilize the PayPal technique for financial connections.

Purchasing Bitcoin Hand-to-Hand

It will be the actual trial of bitcoin. Will people effectively exchange them to and fro? If this can't occur, there can't be a bitcoin economy since retailers will not have the option to utilize it. If retailers can't utilize it, what natural great right? Luckily, this isn't an issue. iPhone is somewhat of a wait, however, a huge number have applications (versatile wallets) that will peruse QR codes and permit you to send bitcoin to whomever you need.

You can likewise show a QR code of your location, or even convey a card in your wallet with your QR code to allow people to send bitcoin to you. Contingent upon what sort of wallet you have, you would then be able to verify whether the bitcoins have been gotten.

In the following area, I will a few central issues about purchasing from Bitcoin Exchanges.

A short history exercise: When people initially fired setting up real business dependent on bitcoin, they utilized the entirety of the instruments accessible to any vendor. They sold with charge card and PayPal. Visas and PayPal have solid purchaser insurance approaches that make it moderately simple for people to demand a chargeback.

Also, evil people understood this and started acquiring bitcoin and afterward eventually mentioning a chargeback. What's more, since bitcoin is a non-actual item, sent by new and inadequately comprehended innovative methods, the dealers couldn't challenge this. Also, merchants quit tolerating Mastercards and PayPal.

Some businesses arose that would acknowledge you for bitcoin if you wired them cash. Regularly these organizations would give addresses in Albania, Poland, or Russia. The truth of the matter is that a considerable lot of this managed job and there are a lot of stories on the discussions of people who purchased bitcoins thusly.

Bitcoin Malpractices That Exist

Bitcoin, the most mainstream crypto that exists is presently considered as perhaps the most famous speculations. Yet, do you realize that this has led to a lot of new bitcoin tricks? Indeed, that is reality and tragically, you can be a piece of it if you know nothing identified with these tricks. This article tells you pretty much every one of the sorts of bitcoin tricks that exist.

Counterfeit trades

One of the most un-troublesome approaches to extortion financial backers is to act as a web advertiser part of a decent and authentic business. However, that is explicitly what con artists inside the bitcoin discipline are doing. Numerous such trades exist and they introduced themselves being a spot to trade and exchange bitcoin, however was in the long run fake. Numerous trades have in this way defrauded people from their cash by essentially acting like another decent and genuine digital money trade.

Phishing Scams

Continuously be keeping watch for phishing cheats. Phishing assaults surely are a top pick among programmers and con artists. Inside a phishing assault, a concerned person commonly imitates assistance, business, or person essentially via email or other content-based correspondence, or by facilitating a phony and manipulative site that appears to be a genuine one. The point is consistently to fool a casualty into uncovering their private tips or sending bitcoin to a location the specific con artist claims.

These sorts of messages regularly seem like they are genuine ones however are phony.

Along with the increment in blockchain-sponsored firms, counterfeit ICOs shot to ubiquity as an approach to back these sorts of new organizations. Nonetheless, given the not directed nature of bitcoin itself, the entryway has been open for a wide range of false exercises. Most ICO fakes occurred through getting financial backers to submit in or through counterfeit ICO sites utilizing counterfeit bitcoin wallets or other crypto wallets, or by showing up as genuine digital currency-based organizations. Many have effectively been blamed for such misbehaviors subsequently it is smarter to confirm such wallets before really choosing to put your cash with them.

If you are into the exchanging business, you probably know at this point that humongous returns are essentially unrealistic with regards to bitcoin exchanging, or crypto exchanging in general. Subsequently, when a merchant attempts to give you the guarantee that your cash will be multiplied inside a particular period, then the most ideal choice in such cases is to avoid such intermediaries however much you can. They will just remove your cash and run and you would be left with only sorrow and regret.

First Option Recovery is the most ideal decision with regards to subsidizing recuperations across the globe. They have top-tier lawyers and lawful consultants who assist them with addressing financial fakes remembering Bitcoin Scams for a regular schedule. Attributable to the numerous years in assistance, they have tackled a wide range of financial issues and recuperated the cash from significant tricks across the world.

Various tricks travel every which way however First Option Recovery consistently stays, in this way continually assisting their customers with recuperating their cash in the speediest, quickest, and best way imaginable. You can reach them for free counsel whenever.

8 Bitcoin Security Tips

Today, with the assistance of Bitcoin, you can change how you do your business. You can easily make installments with the help of virtual cash. Furthermore, you will not need to pay anything to a middle person as there will be no card preparation included.

You have your Bitcoins in your Bitcoin wallet, which will kind of your bank. However, there is a trick. If you lose your wallet key, you will presently don't approach your computerized cash. Additionally, if the critical terrains in the wrong hands, your wallet will be vacant like a flash. Thus, for your security, we propose that you follow the accompanying security tips. Peruse on.

Do not permit open admittance to your Wallet

As per Joe Steward, you ought not to permit open admittance to your Bitcoin wallets. If a representative gets to your wallet and causes an exchange to a wallet they to approach, your cash will be no more. To manage this issue, you can utilize sub-wallets.

Utilize a Reliable Exchange Service

Web wallets are unsafe as programmers use them to acquire unapproved admittance to people's cash. If you truly need to utilize one, ensure you utilize a dependable trade government. When the trade exchange occurs, ensure you move the coins to your wallet immediately.

Use Separate Wallets

Frequently, Bitcoin wallets that are associated with the web constantly are inclined to organize arranged assaults. Thus, it's smart should utilize disconnected wallets, however. In reality, what you need to do is keep your computerized cash in the disconnected wallets. When you get a major measure of cash in your online wallet, ensure you move it to your disconnected wallet straightaway.

Utilize a Dedicated Hardware

It's better if you utilize a committed USB key to move information between two computers.

Store Your Keys Offline

It's a smart thought to store your private keys on a disconnected PC, which will help you avoid programmers and malware as much as possible. However, you need to keep the system as secure as could be expected.

Make Backups

You will lose your Bitcoin or wallet if you wind up harming your PC. Thus, it's a smart idea to make a reinforcement of your wallet another person. **Use Linux for added Security**

If you are searching for the most ideal approach to move information between two computers, you might need to utilize a USB drive. For this reason, the most secure system is Linux as it is truly adept at battling USB-based dangers.

Utilize a Powerful Hardware Wallet

An equipment wallet is a USB key that has a locally available PC that runs an uncommon OS. The equipment keeps the hidden keys secure.

The Bitcoin coal face

Bitcoin mining is the way toward creating Bitcoins. It is also a little installment. This is done using various techniques from utilizing your own PC's CPU or GPU to utilizing ASIC diggers (Application Specific Integrated Circuits), these are intended for the particular reason for which they are fabricated, which for this situation is creating Bitcoins.

Except if you have a critical venture to buy amazing ASIC diggers, for example, those from butterflylabs.com which can run at 600GH/s (Hash's every second) you should take a gander at USB ASIC Miners, for example, the well-known BlockErupter which create 336MH/s. Utilizing the BlockErupters you can make your USB center point style rig running heaps of them simultaneously.

The truth, however, is that it very well might be past the point of no return in the game to bring in any genuine cash from Bitcoin mining. The intricacy (Hash pace) of the BlockChain is currently with the end goal that in any event, joining and adding to a Mining Pool, where excavators cooperate and share the benefits, will probably see more spent in power than in any genuine financial return. Additionally, there is the greatest constraint of 21 million Bitcoins and at present, it is approaching 12.4 million and as more diggers join, the speedier this cutoff will be reached. It is presently more probable you will bring in cash purchasing Bitcoins themselves than producing them.

Important Things to Know About Bitcoin

All think about Bitcoin exchanging. While the vast majority have had accomplishments with the money, others have confronted difficulties. If you are anticipating getting into the market here is a portion of the things you should be careful about:

Paired choices Bitcoin exchanging stage

Paired choices agents are getting comfortable with the ubiquity of these Bitcoins, and their steady fluctuating qualities. Along these lines, they are utilizing this chance to offer dealers the most recent unstable digital money as an extra payment technique.

Is Bitcoin exchanging secure?

Bitcoin network is conceivably the world's huge spread registering project. Bitcoin wallet records can get lost, taken, or erased incidentally actually like some other documents in the advanced structure. You could pick the specialist co-ops who offer significant level security, just as protection against disaster or burglary.

The following are some valid justifications for why it merits utilizing this cryptographic money.

It isn't inflationary - the Federal Reserve prints more dollars, at whatever point the economy is faltering. Government infuses the new-made cash into the economy causing a diminishing in money esteem, accordingly setting off expansion. Swelling diminishes people's ability to purchase things since the costs of merchandise increment.

Modest - Credit or check card exchanges are moments, however, you are charged an expense for utilizing this advantage. In the Bitcoin exchanges, the expenses are normally low, and now and again, it is free.

Fast payments - When payments are made by utilizing banks, the exchange requires a few days, likewise wire moves also take quite a while. Then again, virtual money Bitcoin exchanges are for the most part faster.

"Zero-affirmation" exchanges are momentary, where the dealer acknowledges the danger, which is as yet not endorsed by the Bitcoin block-chain. Assuming the shipper needs an endorsement, the exchange requires 10 minutes. This is substantially more quickly than any between banking move.

People buy merchandise and if they think that it is inadequate, they contact the Mastercards office to make a chargeback, viably switching the exchange. The MasterCard organization does it and accuses you of expensive chargeback expense going from $5-$15.

No chargeback - You can't recover them without the beneficiary's assent. In this manner, it gets hard to submit the chargeback misrepresentation, which is frequently capable by people with Mastercards.

Safe person subtleties - Credit card numbers get taken during the web payments. A Bitcoin exchange needn't bother with any close-to-home subtleties. You must consolidate the Bitcoin key and private key together to do an exchange. And you should guarantee that your reserved key is not gotten to by any outsiders.

Bitcoin's Impact On Currency

Bitcoin is a progressive type of money. It was presented in 2009. It capacities by empowering exchanges to go through without the requirement for the center man. In this way, no banks are required. You also get the advantage of no exchange charges and no need to give out your genuine name. With such adaptability, bitcoin has gotten broadly acknowledged by the two buyers and vendors. It also can be utilized to buy web facilitating administrations, food sources online, and pretty much any help you can consider online.

Bitcoin has affected much on the money field. It is used to buy any stock secretly. It also gives the advantages of simple and modest global payments and isn't oppressed or restricted to any country or guideline. A few groups consider Bitcoin to be a vehicle for ventures and purchase Bitcoin by believing that it will increment in esteem.

To get Bitcoins, you can buy them on an Exchange commercial center that permits people to purchase or sell them, using other different financial forms. The moving of Bitcoins is effectively done by sending Bitcoins to each other person using versatile applications or their PCs online. It's very much like sending cash carefully.

With Bitcoins, you have money esteem that can be put away in what's known as a "digital wallet," which remains alive either inside the cloud or on a PC. This advanced wallet resembles a virtual financial balance that lets account holders inside it send or get Bitcoins, buy labor and products or store them. Albeit most financial balances are safeguarded by the FDIC, Bitcoin wallets are not, yet they are protected, get and have payment adaptability benefits.

In contrast to the gold, US dollar, silver, or any other valuable metals, Bitcoins are scant. And this shortage is algorithmic. As far as global settlement Bitcoin is a champ. There is no stress over extortion or security. At some cash trade organizations, for example, transient specialists could use Bitcoin to send payments starting with one country then onto the next through email.

Things You Should Know About Bitcoin Black

What is Bitcoin Black?

Bitcoin Black is essentially the digital currency of people, by people for people. It will be received for use as a companion 2 friend payment system which gives the force back to people.

If we talk about Bitcoin, Bitcoin has fizzled at this, genuine worth comes from genuine utilization of the biological system and engaging people.

Bitcoin exchanges are moderate and costly, and it tends to be said that Bitcoin is fairly concentrated. Bitcoin takes the force of people since it is vigorously controlled and through cycles that deter members from digital money when all is said in done.

People purchase bitcoin to get rich, not to be engaged with the biological system. The one percent world-class exploits bitcoin and makes demoralization, deliberately expanding the cost and pulling in the section for the fantasy of abundance and unloading coins for their advantage. In dread of selection. Bitcoin is totally controlled, siphoned, and controlled freely, for various reasons.

Bitcoin Black is focusing on tackling these issues as the coin is digital money with a reasonable appropriation Airdropped to 1 Million wallets before IEO which all supports will go to local gatherings cast a ballot by the local area to push the task ahead with center around reasonable dispersion, mass reception, convenience, instruction, straightforward entry, directness, and the local area. The objective is to make it a genuine decentralized independent organization offering the back capacity to people. He doesn't have a place with a gathering, however has a place with numerous parts of the local area.

Appropriation of Coins

Bitcoin Black is intending to have an airdrop to in any event 1 million wallets at first with not over 0.5% of

supply possessed by 1 establishing part making it genuinely decentralized digital currency. The undertaking has a pre-offer of 2.5% of all out supply which is just about 900 Million coins.

If we investigate the IEO, 7.2 billion IEO coins will be designated to a few local area establishments that will help the local area push the undertaking ahead later on. Partner assets for control (around 5%). Part utilized for the solidness control asset to dispose of the chance of early control at low volume and keep up cash strength.

At long last, the awards for presenting the application will be 14.4 billion coins. Presentation of 30 million people with an expansion in the pace of new clients. A strategy for bringing the coin into each schoolyard/college/working environment and the local area.

Does Bitcoin Make Good Sense?

What is the most sizzling innovation improvement of 2013? Most specialists will highlight the ascent of bitcoin. Bitcoin is on the ascent of digital money utilized around the world. It is a kind of cash controlled and put away completely by PCs spread across the Internet. More people and more organizations are beginning to use it. Dissimilar to a plain U.S. dollar or Euro, bitcoin is likewise a type of payment system similar to PayPal or a Visa organization.

You can clutch, spend OR exchange it. It can be moved around effectively practically just like sending an email. Bitcoin lets anyone make exchanges without revealing your personality. However, the system works in plain general visibility. Anybody can see these exchanges which are recorded online. This directness can drive another trust in the economy. It even brought about the ruin of an unlawful medication ring, found rearranging reserves using bitcoin, and shut somewhere near the U.S. Government.

From various perspectives, bitcoin is something beyond cash. It's a re-designing of a worldwide account. It can break down hindrances among nations and liberates money from the control of central governments. Nonetheless, it depends on the U.S. dollar for its worth. The innovation behind this is fascinating no doubt.

Bitcoin is constrained by open-source programming. It works as per the laws of math, and by people who regulate this product. The product runs on a large number of machines around the world, however, it very well may be changed. Changes can happen anyway when most of those supervising the product consent to it.

The bitcoin programming system was worked by software engineers around five years prior and delivered onto the Internet. It was intended to stumble into a huge organization of machines called bitcoin diggers. Fundamentally, bitcoins are simply long advanced addresses and equilibriums, put away in an online record called the "blockchain." But the system configuration empowered the cash to gradually extend and to urge bitcoin diggers to keep the actual system developing.

When the system makes new bitcoins it offers them to the excavators. At present, 25 bitcoins are paid out to the world's excavators around six times each hour. Those rates can change over the long run. Diggers watch bitcoin exchanges through electronic keys. The keys work related to a confounded email address. If they don't make any sense an excavator can dismiss the exchange.

You could do bitcoin mining on your home PC some years ago. In any case, as the cost of bitcoins has shot up, the mining game has transformed into somewhat of a space race. Hand-crafted equipment, proficient players, and fast extending making power have all committed.

Today, the entirety of the PCs competing for those 25 bitcoins perform 5 quintillion numerical computations each second. To place it in context, that is around 150 fold the number of numerical activities as the world's most impressive supercomputer. Also, mining can be quite dangerous. Organizations that form these custom machines regularly charge you for the equipment forthright, and consistently you hang tight for conveyance is a day when it gets more diligently to mine bitcoins. That lessens the measure of cash you can procure.

For what reason do these bitcoins have esteem? It's quite straightforward. They've developed into something that many people need and they're in restricted stock. Even though the system keeps on putting out bitcoins, this will stop when it arrives at 21 million, which was intended to occur in about the year 2140. Bitcoin has entranced numerous in the tech local area. However, if you follow the securities exchange, you know the worth of a bitcoin can vary significantly.

Around the early piece of 2013, it was sold for $13. From that point forward it has hit $900 and keeps on going here and there fiercely consistently. The genuine fate of bitcoin depends substantially more than on the perspectives of a couple of financial backers. In a new meeting on Reddit, Cameron Winklevoss one of the twins engaged with the Facebook claim with Mark Zuckerberg, and an ardent bitcoin financial backer anticipated that one bitcoin could arrive at a worth of $40,000. That is multiple times what it is today.

A more reasonable view recommends that examiners will ultimately cause bitcoin to crash. It doesn't join the capacity to use its cash in the retail climate, apparently an absolute necessity for long-haul achievement. Its wild vacillations likewise make it a tremendous danger for venture purposes. Still, bitcoin pushes the limits of innovation development. Similar to PayPal in its earliest stages, the commercial center should choose if the danger related to this kind of digital money and payment system makes for great long haul marketing prudence.

Become a major part of the Market:

There are a few different ways of turning out to be major parts of the Bitcoin market. The easiest route is to purchase a devoted PC and introduce some Bitcoins mining programming and begin decoding the squares. This cycle is supposed to be the most straightforward way yet it's lethargic. If you need to bring in cash quicker, you need to frame a group. You ought to coordinate a Bitcoin pool containing four to five people. Then you can frame a mining pool and can unscramble the squares quicker than a person can do.

The speediest method to bring in cash through Bitcoins is that you should go directly to the business sectors. Go for the legitimate and solid Bitcoins trades working on the lookout.

You most importantly need to enlist yourself. Join and make account. The, you should react to the affirmations properly. This will stay up with the latest pretty much every one of the functioning loads of Bitcoins. You can exchange bitcoins at any web-based exchanging stage. A few organizations have even begun tolerating payments in bitcoins.

Conclusion:

The best benefit of Bitcoin is its low development peril. Traditional monetary structures experience the evil impacts of expanding and they will overall lose their purchasing power each year, as governments continue using sums working with to enliven the economy. Bitcoin doesn't encounter the evil impacts of low extension, because Bitcoin mining is limited to just 21 million units. That suggests the appearance of new Bitcoins is moving down and all that will be mined out inside the next forever and a day.

More people have recognized the use of Bitcoin and partners believe that one day, the computerized cash will be utilized by purchasers for their web shopping and other digital plans. Critical associations have adequately recognized installments using virtual cash. A part of the huge firms fuses TigerDirect, Fiverr, and Zynga, among others.

Bitcoin works, nonetheless, intellectuals have said that computerized cash isn't fit to be utilized by the norm because of its capriciousness. They additionally highlight the hacking of the Bitcoin exchange the previous that has achieved the inadequacy of a couple of extraordinary numerous dollars. Partners of current financial structures have said that more exceptional exchanges are coordinated by monetary trained professionals and financial backers. Experts added that there is still anticipate virtual cash framework and the expected advancement is titanic.